# NEW EVE

## 30 DEVOTIONS FOR OLDER PEOPLE ... ..AUGHLAN

## God's Unfailing Love

Other *New Every Day* titles
# God's Great Faithfulness

Published 2011 by CWR, Waverley Abbey House, Waverley Lane, Farnham, Surrey GU9 8EP, UK. Registered Charity No. 294387. Registered Limited Company No. 1990308.

For list of National Distributors visit: www.cwr.org/distributors
Unless otherwise marked, all Scripture references are from the Holy Bible: New International Version (NIV), copyright © 1973, 1978, 1984 by the International Bible Society.
Other Scripture version used:
NRSV: New Revised Standard Version, © 1989, by the Division of Christian Education of the National Council of the Churches of Christ in the USA and are used by permission. All rights reserved.
Concept development, editing, design and production by CWR
Cover image: Getty/Stockbyte/Rana Faure
Printed in England by Linney Print
ISBN: 978-1-85345-650-3

# God's great love for us

*H*ow great is the love the Father has lavished on us, that we should be called children of God! God is love. Whoever lives in love lives in God, and God in him. In this way, love is made complete among us so that we will have confidence on the day of judgment, because in this world we are like him. There is no fear in love. But perfect love drives out fear, because fear has to do with punishment. The one who fears is not made perfect in love. We love because he first loved us.
*1 John 3:1; 4:16b–19*

God is love. He loves us because His nature is love and He lavishes that love on us, His children. There is nothing we can do to make God love us more and there is nothing we can do to make Him love us less. We can make God sad or angry but He will never stop loving us.

He calls us His children. What a privilege for us to call Him our Father – such a wise, strong, loving Father! And as we grow up in Him, we too will be loving, able to love as God loves us.

**Prayer:**
**Thank You, Father, for loving me so much. Help me to show Your love today to those I meet. Amen.**

# God's love in Jesus

*T*his is how God showed his love among us: He sent his one and only Son into the world that we might live through him. This is love: not that we loved God but that he loved us and sent his Son as an atoning sacrifice for our sins ...

We know that we live in him and he in us, because he has given us of his Spirit. And we have seen and testify that the Father has sent his Son to be the Saviour of the world. If anyone acknowledges that Jesus is the Son of God, God lives in him and he in God. *1 John 4:9–10,13–15*

Imagine that you have committed a serious crime. You come up before a judge and receive your sentence – guilty! You are given a huge fine, which you cannot pay. But then the judge says, 'I will pay your fine for you. You may go free.'

This is just what God has done for us. Because we have sinned against Him and not always lived our lives as He wants us to, we deserve to be separated from His love. But God sent His Son, Jesus, into the world to take our punishment by giving His life instead of ours on the cross at Calvary.

**Prayer:**
**Thank You, Jesus, for giving Your life for me. Amen.**

# No fear in love

*A*nd so we know and rely on the love God has for us. God is love. Whoever lives in love lives in God, and God in him. In this way, love is made complete among us so that we will have confidence on the day of judgment, because in this world we are like him. There is no fear in love. But perfect love drives out fear, because fear has to do with punishment. The one who fears is not made perfect in love. *1 John 4:16–18*

All of us are going to come to the end of our lives sometime, whether early or late, and we sometimes wonder what will happen afterwards. The Bible tells us that we need have no fear when we trust in the love of God and live in His love. God's love is something we can rely on. That is a very strong and reassuring statement! We will meet Him on the day of judgment and have confidence that we do not face punishment because Jesus has taken our punishment for us.

What wonderful assurance! What a wonderful God we have!

**Prayer:**
**Tell Jesus about any fears or anxieties you have and ask Him to take them away. Let His love fill you through and through. Trust Him with your life; trust in His love.**

# My God, in whom I trust

*Y*ou who live in the shelter of the Most High, who abide in the shadow of the Almighty, will say to the LORD, 'My refuge and my fortress; my God, in whom I trust.' Those who love me, I will deliver; I will protect those who know my name. When they call to me, I will answer them; I will be with them in trouble, I will rescue them and honour them. With long life I will satisfy them, and show them my salvation. *Psalm 91:1–2,14–16 (NRSV)*

So many promises in a few short verses! If we love God and put our trust in Him, we can be sure that He will rescue us from danger, protect us, answer our prayers, be with us in any trouble, deliver us from the enemy and honour us. This psalm is one of the most reassuring scriptures in the whole Bible, giving us a clear picture of God who is utterly reliable, trustworthy and capable. He has promised to answer those who call upon Him.

Ask yourself, 'Do I always remember to call upon Him when I am in need?' He wants you to!

**Prayer:**
**Lord God, please help me to trust You and to call upon You whenever I am in need. Amen.**

# In old age they still produce fruit

*I*t is good to give thanks to the LORD, to sing praises to your name, O Most High; to declare your steadfast love in the morning and your faithfulness by night …

The righteous flourish like the palm tree, and grow like a cedar in Lebanon. They are planted in the house of the Lord; they flourish in the courts of our God. In old age they still produce fruit; they are always green and full of sap, showing that the Lord is upright; he is my rock, and there is no unrighteousness in him.
*Psalm 92:1–2,12–15 (NRSV)*

It is easy to think, as we grow older, that we are losing our usefulness, no longer able to do all the things we used to do when young and active. But the Bible promises us that in old age we will 'still produce fruit'.

The secret is to keep our roots deep down in God, drawing nourishment from Him as we praise Him, read His Word daily, keep in close contact through prayer and remember His love and faithfulness day by day. Then we will be like a strong tree that stands firm and upright in the gale, bearing fruit for Him.

**Prayer:**
**Thank You, Lord, for Your love and faithfulness to me. Help me to be strong and produce fruit for You. Amen.**

# The fruit of the Spirit

*T*he fruit of the Spirit is love, joy, peace, patience, kindness, goodness, faithfulness, gentleness and self-control. Against such things there is no law.
*Galatians 5:22–23*

Think about a fruit tree. Through the year the tree draws nourishment through its roots and responds to the sun on its leaves. As a result of careful tending and pruning by the gardener, a strong tree weathers the winter storms and blossoms in the spring, producing fruit in the late summer or autumn.

As you look back over your life you may remember hard times, times of spiritual drought or hard pruning, as well as good times of joy and great blessing.

Our Father God, the heavenly Gardener, has been looking after you all through the years and, as we read yesterday, He has promised that the righteous will still produce fruit in old age, the autumn of life.

**To think about:**
**Look again at the list of fruit in our reading today. Can you see these in your life? Are there any that are lacking? Ask God to help you show all the fruit of the Spirit in your attitude to others every day.**

# Love never fails

*L*ove is patient, love is kind. It does not envy, it does not boast, it is not proud. It is not rude, it is not self-seeking, it is not easily angered, it keeps no record of wrongs. Love does not delight in evil but rejoices with the truth. It always protects, always trusts, always hopes, always perseveres. Love never fails.
*1 Corinthians 13:4–8a*

At the beginning of this week we read that 'God is love'. So, this passage is a description of God – how He loves and deals with us, His children. He is constant, protective, faithful, persevering and always kind. It is very reassuring to know that once we have said 'sorry' for our sins, God forgives us and does not keep a record of our wrongdoings.

But this scripture is also a description of what we should be like, as we allow the fruit of the Spirit to grow in our lives. God wants us to be like Him, filled with His love. Are there any instances where you feel you fail to be loving? Why not tell God now that you are sorry and accept His forgiveness.

**Prayer:**
**Father, thank You for loving me in such a wonderful way. Please help me to be loving in the same way that You love me. Amen.**

# A life of worship – Anna

*T*here was also a prophetess, Anna, the daughter of Phanuel, of the tribe of Asher. She was very old; she had lived with her husband seven years after her marriage, and then was a widow until she was eighty-four. She never left the temple but worshipped night and day, fasting and praying. Coming up to them [Joseph, Mary and baby Jesus] at that very moment, she gave thanks to God and spoke about the child to all who were looking forward to the redemption of Jerusalem.
*Luke 2:36–38*

Anna had spent her long years of widowhood worshipping in the Temple in Jerusalem, and in her old age she was still faithful to her calling. We are not told if she had arthritic knees by that time – whether she found it difficult to kneel or to stand – that was not important. When Joseph and Mary brought baby Jesus to the Temple to offer a sacrifice and dedicate Him to the Lord as the law required, Anna was ready. She recognised Jesus, the One she had been waiting for all her life, the expected Messiah. She was ready to speak about Him to all who would listen.

We can all do that.

**Prayer:**
**Lord, help me to be faithful as Anna was, and to be ready to speak about You when You give me the opportunities. Amen.**

# Delayed fulfilment – Simeon

*N*ow there was a man in Jerusalem called Simeon, who was righteous and devout. He was waiting for the consolation of Israel, and the Holy Spirit was upon him. It had been revealed to him by the Holy Spirit that he would not die before he had seen the Lord's Christ. Moved by the Spirit, he went into the temple courts. When the parents brought in the child Jesus to do for him what the custom of the Law required, Simeon took him in his arms and praised God, saying: 'Sovereign Lord, as you have promised, you now dismiss your servant in peace.' *Luke 2:25–29*

Simeon, like Anna, had been waiting many years for the revealing of the Christ, the One who would come to save Israel. What a joy it must have been for him when his faith was finally rewarded. Baby Jesus was brought into the Temple and Simeon recognised Him as the long-awaited Messiah.

Sometimes it seems that God is not answering our prayers. Sometimes we wait so long and then give up. But God is always faithful to those who persevere and wait in hope. Simeon waited and trusted that God would fulfil His promise … and God did! Never give up hope.

**Thought:**
**Be encouraged today to persevere in prayer and to wait hopefully and trustingly for God's answer.**

# Letting Go – Moses

*T*hen Moses went out and spoke these words to all Israel: 'I am now a hundred and twenty years old and I am no longer able to lead you.'

Then Moses summoned Joshua and said to him in the presence of all Israel, 'Be strong and courageous, for you must go with this people into the land that the LORD swore to their forefathers to give them ...'

*Deuteronomy 31:1–2a,7*

Moses had been chosen by God to lead the children of Israel out of Egypt and towards the promised land. He had been their leader for forty years, through many difficulties and trials, and although he had made mistakes and disobeyed God on occasion, he had been a strong leader with a close relationship with Him. However, he was not allowed to cross over into Canaan; he had to let go of his position and hand over to a younger man – Joshua.

It is never easy to relinquish something that is close to one's heart. It is not easy to admit that one can no longer cope with the job in hand. Moses was gracious. He was very encouraging to his younger assistant.

**Prayer:**
**Dear Lord, help me to know when to let go and allow others to take over. And help me to let go cheerfully and graciously. Amen.**

# Encouraging the young – David

*D*avid also said to Solomon his son, 'Be strong and courageous, and do the work. Do not be afraid or discouraged, for the LORD God, my God, is with you. He will not fail you or forsake you until all the work for the service of the temple of the LORD is finished.'

Then King David said to the whole assembly: 'My son Solomon, the one whom God has chosen, is young and inexperienced. The task is great, because this palatial structure is not for man but for the LORD God.'
*1 Chronicles 28:20; 29:1*

King David's heart's desire was to build a temple in Jerusalem as a sanctuary for the ark of the covenant. He had made plans and gathered together all the materials needed for a magnificent building. But God would not allow David to build it himself because he was a man of war. The task had to be passed on to his son, Solomon.

It must have been a great disappointment to David not to be able to finish the work but he didn't let it show. Instead he passed the plans to Solomon, encouraged him and validated him before the whole assembly as the one who would carry on the work.

**Prayer:**
**Lord God, please help me to be an encouragement to younger people. Amen.**

# Unselfishness – Paul

*I* would rather appeal to you on the basis of love – and I, Paul, do this as an old man, and now also as a prisoner of Christ Jesus. I am appealing to you for my child, Onesimus, whose father I have become during my imprisonment. Formerly he was useless to you, but now he is indeed useful both to you and to me. I am sending him, that is, my own heart, back to you. I wanted to keep him with me, so that he might be of service to me in your place during my imprisonment for the gospel; but I preferred to do nothing without your consent, in order that your good deed might be voluntary and not something forced. *Philemon 9–14 (NRSV)*

Paul, chained up in a prison in Rome, writes a private letter to his friend, Philemon. One might think Paul would be thinking only about his own problems, but instead he is concerned for others. Onesimus was a slave in Philemon's household and had run away. He reached Rome and there met with Paul and became a follower of Jesus, making himself very useful to Paul.

Instead of keeping the young man for himself, though, Paul sends him back to his master, Philemon. What an unselfish act! Paul puts his friends before his own comfort.

**Prayer:**
**Think about Paul's unselfishness and pray for your friends and family today.**

# Lives of faith – Lois and Eunice

*T*o Timothy, my dear son ... I have been reminded of your sincere faith, which first lived in your grandmother Lois and in your mother Eunice and, I am persuaded, now lives in you also. For this reason I remind you to fan into flame the gift of God, which is in you through the laying on of my hands. For God did not give us a spirit of timidity, but a spirit of power, of love and of self-discipline. *2 Timothy 1:2a,5–7*

Timothy was a young man who was given great responsibility. He had travelled with Paul on his fourth missionary journey and Paul had left him in Ephesus to oversee the church there. Timothy's father was Greek but his mother and grandmother, Eunice and Lois, were Jewish ladies of sincere faith. These two women no doubt taught the young boy from an early age, grounding him in the Scriptures and instilling in him the same faith in God that they had.

Parents and grandparents can have a great influence on a young child's future, preparing them for whatever God calls them to do in later life. God can use us for the next generation's future.

**Prayer:**
**Father, please show me how to pray for the children in my family and to take opportunities to teach them about Jesus. Amen.**

# Faithfulness under persecution – John

*I*, John, your brother and companion in the suffering and kingdom and patient endurance that are ours in Jesus, was on the island of Patmos because of the word of God and the testimony of Jesus. On the Lord's Day I was in the Spirit, and I heard behind me a loud voice like a trumpet, which said: 'Write on a scroll what you see and send it to the seven churches: to Ephesus, Smyrna, Pergamum, Thyatira, Sardis, Philadelphia and Laodicea.' *Revelation 1:9–11*

The book of Revelation was written during a time of intense persecution for Christians. John, by now a very old man, was imprisoned on the island of Patmos. However, his faith in Jesus was as strong as ever, and he remained convinced that God's plan would eventually triumph over the evil forces in the world.

Writing under the direction of the Holy Spirit, John's message to the Church is one of warning that wickedness and persecution will increase, but also of encouragement that in the end Satan will be defeated and 'all things will become new'. John's life of obedience, steadfastness and faithfulness is one which should inspire us to unwavering faith in God.

**Prayer:**
**Please help me, Lord, to have faith in You and remain faithful to You no matter what happens in the world outside. Amen.**

## ... when you feel anxious

*C*ast your cares on the LORD and he will sustain you; he will never let the righteous fall.
*Psalm 55:22*

**Humble yourselves, therefore, under God's mighty hand, that he may lift you up in due time. Cast all your anxiety on him because he cares for you.** *1 Peter 5:6–7*

Your heavenly Father cares for you. He cares about you; He knows all about your life; He knows what you are thinking, what you are anxious about and He longs to help you. So, tell Him about all the things that concern you.

The word 'cast' has several meanings, but perhaps the most helpful in this context is 'throw off, get rid of' (*The Concise Oxford Dictionary*). God wants us to get rid of our anxieties by telling Him about them, one by one, and trusting Him to take care of them. Throw them at Him! Sometimes we will see a solution; sometimes He will send someone to help; sometimes we will just know peace even though the situation doesn't change. But always we can trust our Father to take care of us.

**Action:**
**Tell God every day about anything that causes you anxiety. Believe that He will take care of you. Trust Him and receive His peace.**

## ... when you are worried

'*Therefore do not worry, saying, "What will we eat?" or "What will we drink?" or "What will we wear?" For it is the Gentiles who strive for all these things; and indeed your heavenly Father knows that you need all these things. But strive first for the kingdom of God and his righteousness, and all these things will be given to you as well. So do not worry about tomorrow, for tomorrow will bring worries of its own. Today's trouble is enough for today.' Matthew 6:31–34 (NRSV)*

Jesus was so practical and down to earth in His teaching. He knew exactly what His hearers were like because He lived amongst them, listened to them, ate with them, walked with them. These verses are part of His sermon given to the crowds on the mountain near Capernaum overlooking Lake Galilee. There would have been folk there worried about feeding their families, getting a job, concerned about their health and above all about the Roman occupation of their country. Jesus reassured them that their heavenly Father knew about all these things.

Worry is useless. It does not achieve anything. Live a day at a time, keep your mind on God, and trust Him to look after you.

**Prayer:**
**Father, forgive me for worrying. Please keep me in Your perfect peace and help me to keep my thoughts on You. Amen.**

# ... when you are weary

'*C*ome to me, all you who are weary and burdened, and I will give you rest. Take my yoke upon you and learn from me, for I am gentle and humble in heart, and you will find rest for your souls. For my yoke is easy and my burden is light.' *Matthew 11:28–30*

Jesus links the word 'weary' with 'burdened'. Ordinary tiredness is different; it can be cured by a good night's sleep, or several if necessary. Weariness, though, seems to go on day after day and is often associated with cares and problems in life. And when we are weary the problems seem bigger and impossible to solve.

Yokes are an old fashioned way of making burdens easier. Milkmaids carried their churns across their shoulders with a yoke. Yokes were specially made to fit the oxen as they ploughed the fields. Jesus is saying that if we take *His* yoke, only tackling the work and problems that *He* allows in our lives, not taking on any others, then our burdens will be light and easily borne.

**Prayer:**
**Lord Jesus, thank You for Your teaching. I lay down all my burdens at Your feet today and ask that You show me what to do and what not to do so, that I do not grow weary. Amen.**

## ... when you feel weak

*I* love you, O LORD, my strength. The LORD is my rock, my fortress and my deliverer; my God is my rock, in whom I take refuge. He is my shield and the horn of my salvation, my stronghold ...

It is God who arms me with strength and makes my way perfect. *Psalm 18:1–2,32*

God's strength is infinite. He is unshakable, immovable, completely trustworthy. He is a rock to stand on, a fortress to run into, a deliverer from all ills. He is a shield from all enemies, the strength behind your salvation, a stronghold.

It is *this* God who gives His people strength. It is *this* God who will give you the strength that you need day by day, whether it be spiritual, physical or mental. King David, who wrote this psalm, was troubled by many enemies during his life, but he knew the secret of trusting God to give him the strength to see him through each situation. This same God will give you strength every day for whatever He wants you to do.

**Prayer:**
**Dear God, You know how weak I sometimes feel.**
**I ask You to give me the strength to cope with every**
**situation in my life. Amen.**

# ... when you feel old

*T*herefore we do not lose heart. Though outwardly we are wasting away, yet inwardly we are being renewed day by day. For our light and momentary troubles are achieving for us an eternal glory that far outweighs them all. So we fix our eyes not on what is seen, but on what is unseen. For what is seen is temporary, but what is unseen is eternal.
*2 Corinthians 4:16–18*

Creaking bones, aching muscles, eyesight and hearing failing – all these may be experienced in varying degrees as we grow older. Inevitably, too, in later years we begin to lose friends and loved ones as they pass on before us to greater glory. It is easy to get downhearted about the passing years. Paul, though, encourages the Christians in Corinth to take their eyes off the temporary troubles of this world and instead to concentrate on the eternal truth of the glory that awaits them. And not only future bliss, but the glory they can experience now, being inwardly renewed daily as they fix their eyes on Jesus.

So, take heart and stay cheerful. God is taking care of you now in this life and there is unimaginable joy and delight to look forward to in the next.

**To think about:**
**We live by faith, not by sight. (2 Corinthians 5:7)**

# ... when you feel doubtful

*I*n all my prayers for all of you, I always pray with joy because of your partnership in the gospel from the first day until now, being confident of this, that he who began a good work in you will carry it on to completion until the day of Christ Jesus. *Philippians 1:4–6*

The apostles said to the Lord, 'Increase our faith!' He replied, 'If you have faith as small as a mustard seed, you can say to this mulberry tree, "Be uprooted and planted in the sea," and it will obey you.' *Luke 17:5–6*

The apostles were afraid that their faith was not great enough to do what Jesus expected of them. They made a mistake in thinking that they needed great faith.

What we all actually need is faith in a great God. God is able to keep us, to complete His work in us by His greatness, His power, His might. It is when we rely on our own abilities or start dwelling on all the problems in the world that doubt creeps in. The secret is to look to God, who is almighty and is able to carry us through until we meet with Him face to face.

Prayer:
Father God, I am confident that You have begun a good work in me and that You will complete it. Amen.

# ... when you feel troubled

'*D*o not let your hearts be troubled. Trust in God; trust also in me.'

'All this I have spoken while still with you. But the Counsellor, the Holy Spirit, whom the Father will send in my name, will teach you all things and will remind you of everything I have said to you. Peace I leave with you; my peace I give you. I do not give to you as the world gives. Do not let your hearts be troubled and do not be afraid.'
*John 14:1,25–27*

Jesus spoke these words to His disciples after He had told them He was leaving them. He knew what awaited Him and was preparing them for the horror of His arrest and death. They didn't understand. They were perplexed, troubled and afraid. Jesus understood how they were feeling and gently reassured them, giving them His peace. He still knows and understands just how you feel when you are troubled about anything, and His words are for you just as much as they were for His friends, the disciples. Take them into your heart and receive His peace. Don't be afraid. Trust in God.

**Jesus said:**
**'In this world you will have trouble. But take heart! I have overcome the world.' (John 16:33)**
**Think about these words and thank Jesus for His peace.**

# Confidence

*S*ince, then, we have a great high priest who has passed through the heavens, Jesus, the Son of God, let us hold fast to our confession. For we do not have a high priest who is unable to sympathise with our weaknesses, but we have one who in every respect has been tested as we are, yet without sin. Let us therefore approach the throne of grace with boldness, so that we may receive mercy and find grace to help in time of need. *Hebrews 4:14–16 (NRSV)*

Jesus knows all about our weaknesses because He lived on earth as a man. He experienced life in this world with its problems, sadness and temptations so is able to sympathise with us in any situation that we may go through. What a wonderful thought – that whatever we bring to Jesus in prayer He understands and is there to console and to help. He is our Saviour and Friend as well as the Son of God, our great High Priest in heaven.

So we can approach Him with confidence. When we are tempted, we can ask for strength to overcome. If we fail, we can ask for forgiveness. He is there to help always.

**Prayer:**
**I thank You so much, Lord, that You understand me, that You sympathise with my weaknesses and You are always there to help. Amen.**

# Pray with joy

*B*e joyful always; pray continually; give thanks in all circumstances, for this is God's will for you in Christ Jesus. *1 Thessalonians 5:16–18*

**Rejoice in the Lord always.** *Philippians 4:4*

Think about the first three words of these scriptures, 'Be joyful always …' You might think that this is totally impossible and unreasonable. We all go through periods of sadness in our lives and we can see much to make us unhappy in the world around us. But the second scripture makes sense of the first. We can rejoice *in the Lord* all the time; rejoice and be thankful for what God has done for us through Jesus, giving thanks for His love, His mercy, His forgiveness, His care for us. There is a difference between happiness and joy. Happiness depends on circumstances. Joy comes from deep within us – it is difficult to find sometimes but through prayer, thankfulness and a knowledge of God's presence we can indeed 'rejoice *in the Lord* always'.

**Prayer:**
**Thank You, Father, for Your love for me. Thank You for sending Jesus to die on the cross for me. Thank You for all the beauty of Your creation, for my family and friends – for all Your provision for me. Thank You for joy. Amen.**

# Persevere in prayer

'*A*sk, and it will be given to you; search, and you will find; knock, and the door will be opened for you. For everyone who asks receives, and everyone who searches finds, and for everyone who knocks, the door will be opened. Is there anyone among you who, if your child asks for bread, will give a stone? Or if the child asks for a fish, will give a snake? If you then, who are evil, know how to give good gifts to your children, how much more will your Father in heaven give good things to those who ask him!** *Matthew 7:7–11 (NRSV)*

Jesus is encouraging His listeners here to come as children in prayer to their Father. Children are persistent when they want something badly enough – they keep on asking! The sense of the Greek language in which this Gospel was originally written emphasises this meaning; ask and go on asking, seek and continue seeking, knock persistently until the door is opened. It is not that God doesn't hear our prayer the first time we ask but that He wants us to trust Him, to demonstrate our faith, to keep holding on to that good thing we are asking for.

So, never give up. Keep on praying.

**Action:**
**Think today about what you really want to ask God for … and persevere in prayer day by day.**

# In everything

*D*o not be anxious about anything, but in everything, by prayer and petition, with thanksgiving, present your requests to God. And the peace of God, which transcends all understanding, will guard your hearts and your minds in Christ Jesus.
*Philippians 4:6–7*

There is nothing we cannot talk over with God. Are there things you are anxious or worried about? Tell your heavenly Father about them. Sometimes just chatting things over with God without actually asking for anything will help to calm your mind and set your heart at rest. Other times you need to be specific in your requests. Ask Him to give you peace in circumstances that you cannot change. Ask for wisdom if you have decisions to make. Ask for practical help with tasks you find difficult. Pray for any members of your family you are concerned about, for neighbours, for situations in your locality or nation. Remember, the scripture says 'everything'! There is nothing too small or too big to bring to God in prayer.

**Action:**
**Make a list today of things that concern you. Then take each one to God in prayer with thankfulness for His mighty power and His care.**

# Pray for those in authority

*I* urge, then, first of all, that requests, prayers, intercession and thanksgiving be made for everyone – for kings and all those in authority, that we may live peaceful and quiet lives in all godliness and holiness. This is good and pleases God our Saviour, who wants all men to be saved and to come to a knowledge of the truth. *1 Timothy 2: 1–4*

Timothy was in charge of the church at Ephesus. Paul writes to him to give instructions for the people in the church. His emphasis in this passage is on the importance of prayer for those in authority. How often do we grumble about our government and how often do we pray for the men and women who make the decisions that affect our lives?

Suggestions for prayer: thanksgiving for our democratic government, our freedom to vote, for men and women of goodwill in leadership, for our freedom to worship. Pray for our Prime Minister and government, your own MP, your local councillors, police chiefs, magistrates and judges. Ask for righteousness, for wise decisions, for justice and for godliness, that we may be able to live our lives in peace.

**Prayer:**
Lord God, please show me who You want me to pray for each day. Amen.

# Pray for church leaders

*D*evote yourselves to prayer, being watchful and thankful. And pray for us, too, that God may open a door for our message, so that we may proclaim the mystery of Christ, for which I am in chains. Pray that I may proclaim it clearly, as I should. *Colossians 4:2–4*

As retired people, we have more time to devote to prayer than we had in our working lives. It is good to set aside a specific time each day to read God's Word, to pray with thanksgiving, praise and worship and to bring those requests to Him that He lays on our hearts. In this letter, Paul is asking for prayer for himself and all those who proclaim the gospel message. We can pray for our own local ministers, youth leaders, Sunday School teachers and church workers. Then, looking into the wider world, we can pray for evangelists and missionaries in countries where it is more difficult to preach the good news of the gospel.

What a privilege to be able to bring these requests to God, that the gospel may be preached clearly and reach those who need to hear throughout the world.

**Prayer:**
**Father God, thank You for men and women who proclaim Your good news. I ask You today to bless and strengthen my own church leaders. Amen.**

# For all God's people

*A*nd pray in the Spirit on all occasions with all kinds of prayers and requests. With this in mind, be alert and always keep on praying for all the saints. Pray also for me, that whenever I open my mouth, words may be given me so that I will fearlessly make known the mystery of the gospel, for which I am an ambassador in chains. Pray that I may declare it fearlessly, as I should. *Ephesians 6:18–20*

Paul also encourages his readers to pray 'for all the saints', by which he means God's people everywhere, all those who believe in Jesus. Saints do not just live in stained-glass windows or statues. They are you and me and the folk we know who love the Lord – your friends in your church and Christians throughout the world. There are countries in the world where the Church is growing, and others where the Church is persecuted where it is very hard to be a Christian. God knows and cares for each one of His people and He asks you to care, too, and to pray for them. Perhaps you could choose one particular country and pray regularly for the Christians there.

**Prayer:**
**Father, I ask You to strengthen Your people who are suffering hardship, persecution or ridicule for Your sake. Be with them, Lord, and comfort them. Amen.**

# Praying for God's people

*A*nd this is my prayer: that your love may abound more and more in knowledge and depth of insight, so that you may be able to discern what is best and may be pure and blameless until the day of Christ, filled with the fruit of righteousness that comes through Jesus Christ – to the glory and praise of God. *Philippians 1:9–11*

Sometimes we know exactly how to pray for folk we know well. We know what they are going through and what they need. It is easy to pray. For people we don't know, however, or have not had contact with for some time, it is good to turn to the Scriptures for some advice. Paul's prayer for those in the church at Philippi is a good example that we can follow. He asks:

- that their love may abound;
- that their knowledge and insight may increase so that they can discern what is best;
- that they may be pure and blameless until Jesus comes again;
- that their lives will bear the fruit of righteousness.

**Prayer:**
**Almighty God, I ask that Your love may abound in my family and in the Church. Please help us to show our love for You by living as You want us to. Amen.**

# Praise

*S*hout for joy to the LORD, all the earth. Worship the LORD with gladness; come before him with joyful songs. Know that the LORD is God. It is he who has made us, and we are his; we are his people, the sheep of his pasture. Enter his gates with thanksgiving and his courts with praise; give thanks to him and praise his name. For the LORD is good and his love endures forever; his faithfulness continues through all generations. *Psalm 100*

At the end of these thirty days of readings, we come to the Lord with worship and praise. This psalm reminds us of several things about God:

*He is the Creator and He made us.*
*We belong to Him and we are His.*
*He is good.*
*His love lasts forever.*
*He has always been faithful and He always will be.*

**Response:**
**So consider afresh God's mighty works, His love for you and His care for you. Spend some time thanking Him for all the blessings you have experienced over the years. Praise Him for the wonders of creation and for His majesty, power and might.**

**You may like to sing a hymn of praise or just speak aloud your praise to our loving, faithful Creator God.**